ONENOTE

FOR BEGINNERS

2023

YOUR PATHWAY TO EFFICIENT NOTE-TAKING
AND ORGANIZATIONAL EXCELLENCE!

By

Dennis Charles

COPYRIGHT

Printed in the United States of America
© 2023 by Dennis Charles

New Age Publishing
USA | UK | CANADA

TABLE OF CONTENTS

INTRODUCTION

Did you know that over 85% of workers need help keeping their information and notes in order? We are exposed to more and more data daily, so it's unsurprising that it can be hard to keep track of it all. But don't worry! In this book, we'll learn more about OneNote, a powerful program that will change how you keep track of your tasks and organize your notes. This book is the best way to learn how to use OneNote, whether you are a student, a worker, or just someone who wants to get more done.

Chapter 1: How to Use OneNote for the First Time

- Find out how to get OneNote and put it on your device.

- Learn how to use OneNote by getting to know its interface and simple functions.

- Find out how to make notebooks, parts, and pages and organize them.

Chapter 2: How to Take Notes Like a Pro

- Learn about the different tools and functions in OneNote for taking notes.

- Try different ways to take notes using tags, audio files, and pictures.

- Find out how to arrange your notes using sections, pages, and subpages.

Chapter 3: Managing your notes

- Find out how to export notebooks in different formats.

- Look into advanced ways to secure your notes and use page templates.

Chapter 4: Working together and giving to others

- Check out the shared features of OneNote, like co-authoring and sharing in real-time.

- Find out how to let other people use your notes and limit their access.

- Find out how to connect OneNote to other Microsoft Office programs so you can work together efficiently.

Chapter 5: Tips and Tricks for Pros

- Find out how to use OneNote's time-saving shortcuts.

- Learn about advanced features like transforming images into text.

- Find out how to change OneNote to fit your needs and how you work.

And lots of exercises.

Conclusion:

By the end of this book, you will know a lot about OneNote and what it can do. This will give you more power than ever over your notes and information. Say goodbye to papers that are all over the place and ideas you can't find. With OneNote, all your notes and ideas will be in one place where they are easy to find and organized. Get ready for OneNote to help you get more done and be more productive. So, why don't you do it? Let's dive in and find out how to use OneNote to its fullest!

CHAPTER 1 → A BRIEF LOOK AT ONENOTE

In this section, we'll tell you everything you need to know about OneNote, including what it is and how it can help you. We will talk about the essential ideas and features of OneNote. This will give you a solid base to build on throughout the rest of the book.

WHAT DOES ONENOTE DO?

OneNote is a program made by Microsoft for taking digital notes.

It lets users make notes in text, images, audio, and other forms, organize them, and share them.

OneNote is a powerful tool for both personal and business use because it lets you capture and organize information in a flexible and easy way.

OneNote's Most Important Parts

OneNote has a lot of tools that make it easier to take notes and organize them. These things are:

- Notebooks: Keep your notes organized by putting them in different notebooks.

- Sections and Pages: To keep your notes more organized, divide your papers into sections and pages.

- Formatting options: You can change the way your notes look by using tools like fonts, colors, and styles to change the way they look.

- Tags: You can add tags to your notes to highlight important information or point out things that need to be done.

- Search: It's easy to look through your notes for specific words or sentences.

- Syncing and Cloud Storage: You can access your notes from different devices and keep them in sync using cloud storage services.

- Collaboration: Share your notebooks with other people and work on projects or papers together in real-time.

Why you should use OneNote?

- Better organization: OneNote gives you a place to store and organize your notes that is structured and easy to find.

This means you no longer need physical notebooks or scattered digital files.

- Better productivity: With features like tags, search, and tools for working together, OneNote makes it easier to take notes and helps you stay on track and get things done.

- Accessibility and synchronization: You can access your notes from any device with an internet link, and they will be the same on all of them.

- Flexibility and customization: OneNote gives you a lot of choices for how to format your notes, so you can make them your own and set up a system that works best for you.

- Integration with Microsoft Office: OneNote works well with other Microsoft Office programs like Outlook and Word, making them more productive and easier to do things smoothly.

How to Use OneNote for the First Time

- How to Download and Install OneNote: Find out how to download and install OneNote on Windows, Mac, iOS, and Android platforms.

Setting up OneNote: Learn how to set it up for the first time and make a new notebook.

- Using the OneNote Interface: Get to know the different parts of the OneNote interface, like the ribbon, the navigation bar, and the page tabs.

By the end of this section, you'll know what OneNote is, its most important features, and how to start using the app. You'll be ready to learn more about OneNote and use it to its fullest extent. So, let's dive in and discover what's so interesting about OneNote.

WHY YOU SHOULD USE ONENOTE

In this section, we'll go into more detail about the benefits of using OneNote as a digital note-taking tool. We will look at how OneNote can help you stay more organized, be more productive, be easier to use, give you more options, and work well with other Microsoft Office programs.

Better Organizing

One of the best things about using OneNote is that it gives you a place to store and organize your notes that is organized and easy to find. You no longer have to look through actual notebooks or scattered digital files to find what you need. With OneNote, you can make multiple notebooks to organize your notes by topic, divide them into parts and pages, and add tags to highlight important information or remind you to do something. This level of organization makes it easy to find specific notes or topics quickly, which saves time and makes you more productive.

Better Work Outcomes

OneNote has a lot of tools that make it easier to take notes and help you stay on task and get things done. With choices like fonts, colors, and styles, you can change how your notes look to suit your tastes. The search feature makes it easy to find specific words or sentences in your notes, so you don't have to look through them all by hand. OneNote also has tools that let you share your notebooks with others and work on shared projects or papers simultaneously. This feature makes people more productive, especially when working on group projects or tasks.

Getting Access and Syncing

No longer are people tied to a single item or place. Using OneNote, you can get to your notes from any internet-connected device. You can download and run OneNote on a Windows computer, a Mac, an iOS device, or an Android device, and your notes will be the same on all of them. This means you can start taking notes on your laptop and then continue right where you left off on your phone or tablet. OneNote's accessibility and sharing features make it easy and flexible for people to take notes on the go.

Ability to change and adapt

OneNote gives you a lot of ways to arrange your notes, so you can make them your own and make a system that works best for you. Whether you like bullet points, numbered lists, tables, or pictures in your notes, OneNote gives you the tools you need to make them fit your needs. You can also add audio clips, files, or hyperlinks to your notes, which makes them even more detailed and interactive. Because OneNote is flexible and can be changed, you can make a note-taking system that fits how you learn or work. This will make your total experience with OneNote better.

Linking to Microsoft Office

OneNote works well with other Microsoft Office programs like Outlook and Word because it is part of the Microsoft Office suite. This integration improves productivity by making it possible for different Microsoft Office apps to work together smoothly. For instance, you can easily share notes from OneNote to Outlook. This lets you turn your notes into tasks or calendar events that you can do. You can also import content straight from Word documents into OneNote, which saves you time and work. OneNote is a potent tool for people who take notes and use other Microsoft programs for work or school. It works well with Microsoft Office.

By the end of this section, you will know everything there is to learn about the benefits of using OneNote. You will have the knowledge and desire to use OneNote to its full potential for taking notes. So let's keep exploring the exciting world of OneNote and find out how to use it to its fullest!

HOW TO SET UP ONENOTE

In this section, we'll show you how to set up OneNote on your computer. We will give you step-by-step steps for installing and setting up the app on a Windows computer, a Mac, an iOS device, or an Android device.

Microsoft

Follow these steps to set up OneNote on a computer running Windows:

Step 1: On your Windows PC, go to the Microsoft Store and open it.

Step 2: Type "OneNote" into the search bar to find it.

Step 3: Click the OneNote app in the list of results from your search.

Step 4: Click "Get" or "Install" to get OneNote downloaded and set up on your computer.

Step 5: Launch OneNote from the Start menu or the desktop once the download is done.

Mac

Here's how Mac users can set up OneNote:

Step 1: On your Mac, open the App Store.

Step 2: Type "OneNote" into the search bar to find it.

Step 3: Click the OneNote app in the list of results from your search.

Step 4: Click "Get" or "Install" to get OneNote for your Mac and install it.

Step 5: Once the download is done, you can open OneNote from the Launchpad or the Applications folder.

iOS

Follow these steps to set up OneNote on an iOS device like an iPhone or iPad:

Step 1: On your iOS device, open the App Store.

Step 2: Type "OneNote" into the search bar to find it.

Step 3: Tap the OneNote app in the list of results from your search.

Step 4: Tap the "Get" or "Install" button to download and install OneNote on your computer.

Step 5: Start OneNote from the home screen once the download is done.

Google

Here's how Android users can set up OneNote:

Step 1: On your Android device, open the Google Play Store.

Step 2: Type "OneNote" into the search bar to find it.

Step 3: Tap the OneNote app in the search results list.

Step 4: Tap the "Install" button to download OneNote and set it up on your device.

Step 5: Open OneNote from the app drawer once the download is done.

Now that you've successfully installed OneNote on your device, it's time to set up your account and customize your settings. When you first open OneNote, it will ask you to sign in with your Microsoft account. You can make a free Microsoft account if you don't already have one.

Once signed in, you can check out all of OneNote's features and tools. Learn how to use the interface, make notebooks, parts, and pages, and then start taking your first digital notes.

In the next section, we'll look at the OneNote design in more depth and show you how to use the app well. So, stay tuned and get ready to see how OneNote can help you take notes.

NAVIGATING THE ONENOTE INTERFACE

Once you've successfully loaded OneNote on your device and set up your account, it's time to get to know the app's interface and learn how to use it well.

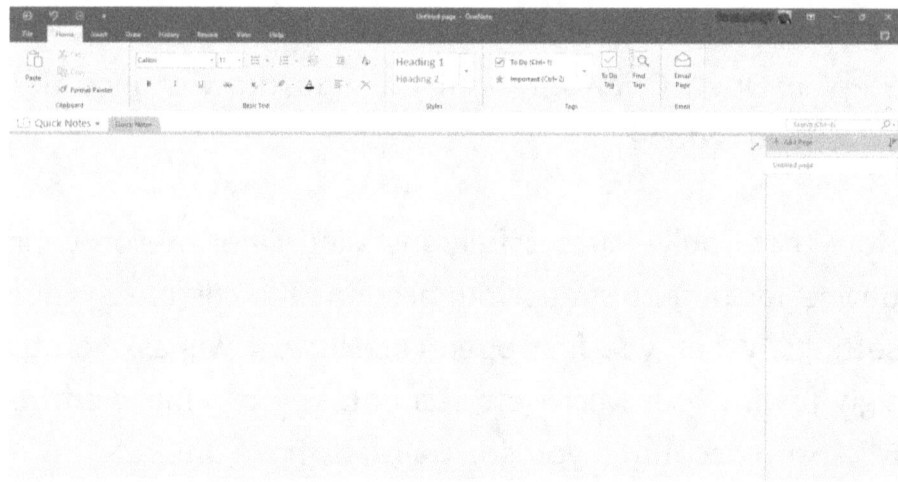

How to Use OneNote's User Interface:

When you open OneNote, you'll see a clean, easy-to-understand layout. Let's look at the different parts of the system more closely:

1. Title Bar: The title bar is at the top of the window and shows the notebook's name, area, and page you are on. It also has buttons to make the app smaller, make it bigger, and close it.

2. Ribbon: The ribbon is a toolbar that sits below the title bar and has different tabs for different tools and tasks. Home, Insert, Draw, History, Review, and View are some of the buttons here. The ribbon makes it easy to access all of OneNote's features and functions.

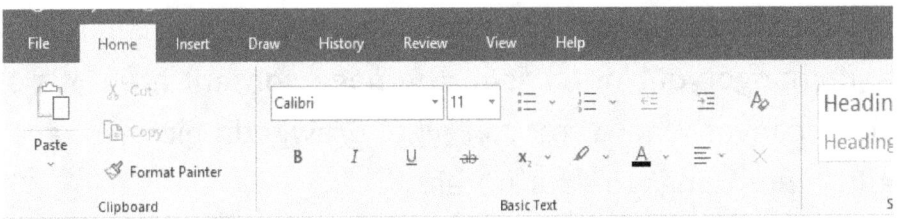

3. Quick Access Toolbar: The quick access toolbar is in the top left area of the window. It gives you quick access to commands like Save, Undo, and Redo. You can change this menu to suit your needs by adding or taking away commands.

4. Navigation Pane: The navigation pane is on the right side of the window. It shows your notebooks, parts, and pages in a tree-like structure. You can make each level bigger or smaller to make it easy to move through your notes.

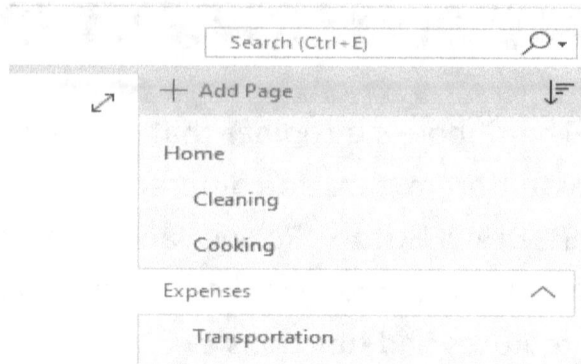

6. Page Content Area: The main place where you can make and change your notes is in the page content area. It's a clean canvas where you can type, draw, add pictures, and add other things to your notes.

How to Move Around in OneNote:

Now that you know how the layout works, let's go over how to move around in OneNote:

1. How to Switch Notebooks, Sections, and Pages:

– Click on the notebook's name in the notebook title bar to switch between them.

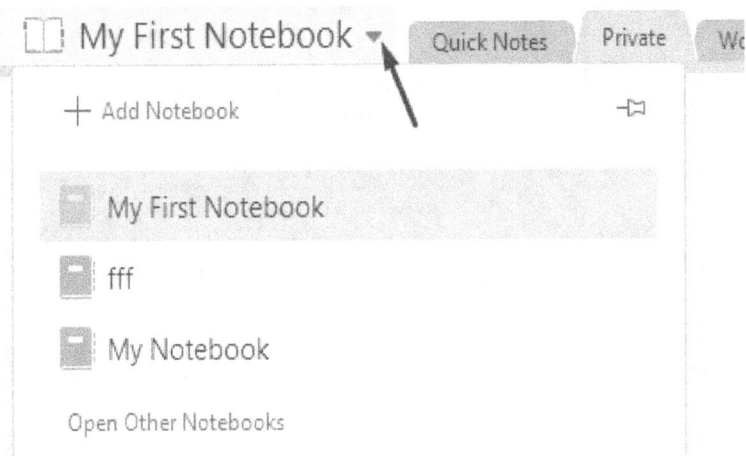

- Click on the name of a section in the notebook title bar to move to that section in a notebook.

- Click on the page tab at the navigation pane to move between pages and subpages within an area.

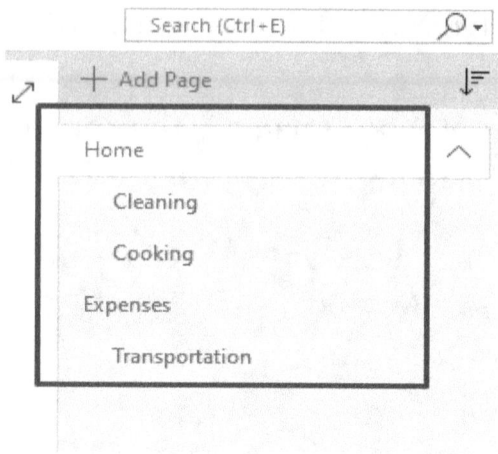

2. How to Scroll and Zoom:

- Use the scroll wheel on your mouse to move up or down a page.

- Hold down the Ctrl key and move the mouse wheel to zoom in or out.

3. To use Search:

- Click on the search bar in the top right of the window to look for something specific in your notes.

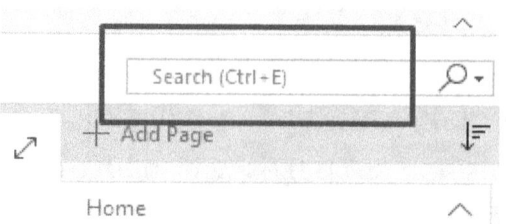

4. How to use Quick Notes:

OneNote lets you write down thoughts or notes quickly without having to look through your notebooks. Press Ctrl+Shift+N to open the Quick Notes window.

- You can type or copy and paste your notes into the Quick Notes window and save them to a specific notebook or area later.

If you know how to use OneNote's navigation and layout, you can organize your notes well and get to them whenever needed. In the next section, we'll take a closer look at the different features and tools that OneNote has to help you take better notes. So, stay tuned and get ready to use OneNote to show off your talent!

CUSTOMIZING ONENOTE FOR YOUR NEEDS

In this section, we'll look at the different ways you can change OneNote to fit your wants and tastes. One of the best things about using OneNote is its flexibility, so you can change it to match your process and style.

Changing the settings for the app:

OneNote has many options that you can change to make your experience better. To get to the settings, hit "File" in the ribbon and then "Options." Here are some of the most important settings you can change:

- General Settings: You can change the default size, language, and measurement units on the General tab. You can also choose whether your notebooks will sync immediately or whether you will be asked to do it yourself.

- Backup and Restore: On the Save & Backup tab, you can set your notes to back up automatically and choose how often they back up. This ensures your notes are safe and sound in case something terrible happens.

- Audio and Video: If you often use audio or video files in your notes, you can change the audio and video settings in the Audio & Video tab. Here, you can choose the default camera and microphone, as well as the quality of the video.

Changing the look of the interface:

OneNote lets you change the way the interface looks to fit your needs. Here are some things to think about:

- Theme: To change how OneNote looks, go to the View tab in the ribbon and choose a theme from the "Page Color" dropdown menu. You can choose from several themes that have already been made, or you can make your own.

- Page templates: If you make a lot of similar pages, you can save time by using page templates. To get to the templates, go to the Insert tab in the ribbon and click on "Page Templates." Choose a template that fits your needs, and it will be added to the present section.

- Quick Access Toolbar: As we've already said, the Quick Access Toolbar makes it easy to use commands you use often. You can change this toolbar to fit your needs by adding or removing the items most important to you. To change the toolbar's appearance, right-click on it and choose "Customize Quick Access Toolbar."

How to Use Labels and Tags:

Tags and labels are vital tools in OneNote that help you organize and classify your notes in the best way possible. To get to the tags, go to the Home tab in the menu and click "Tags." Here are some ways you can use tags and labels:

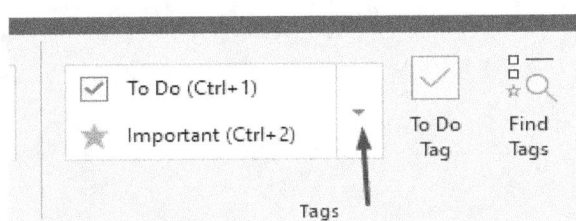

- Setting priorities: Use tags like "Important" or "Urgent" to immediately bring attention to notes that need it. This helps you stay on task and ensure you remember to do everything important.

- Categorizing: Create custom tags for different categories like "Work," "Personal," and "Research." This makes it easy to filter and search for specific types of notes.

- To-Do Lists: OneNote has several tags that can be used to make lists of things to do. To stay organized and on top of your tasks, you can mark items as "Completed," set due dates, or even add reminder notifications.

By changing OneNote to fit your needs, you can make taking notes more accessible and efficient. In the next chapter, we'll look at some of the more advanced features of OneNote that will help you take better notes. So, keep reading to learn how to get the most out of OneNote.

CHAPTER 2 → CREATING AND ORGANIZING NOTES

Now that you know what OneNote is and how it works, let's start making a new notebook.

CREATING A NEW NOTEBOOK

Open OneNote on your computer or device to get started. When you open the program, you will see the main interface, which is made up of sections and pages.

Click on the "File" tab in the top left area of the interface to make a new notebook. There will be a dropdown option. Choose "New" from this menu and then "Notebook."

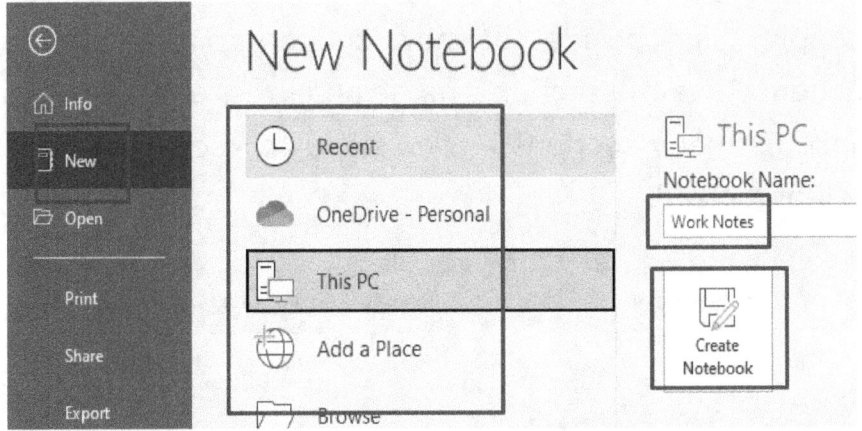

You'll see a box that asks you what you want to call your new notebook. Pick a name that is easy to remember. For example, if you are making a notebook for work, you could call it "Work Notes." Once you have entered the name you want, click "Create" to move on.

Congratulations! You have successfully made a new file in OneNote. Now, let's look at the different features and choices that this notebook gives you.

Organizing your notebook

Now that you have a new notebook, you need to know how to arrange your notes. OneNote gives you different ways to organize and group your knowledge.

Sections: You can make sections in a notebook to separate your content into different groups or areas. By default, there is a section in the new notebook you created. Click the plus sign beside the new section to create more sections. Give the section a name and press enter. You can make as many sections as you need to keep your notes well-organized.

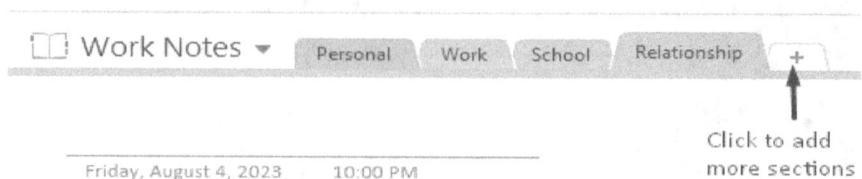

Pages: You can make more than one page in each section to better organize your notes. To create a new page, click the section you want the new page. On the navigation pane, click "Add Page". Right-click a page and choose "Rename" to give the page a title that tells what it is about. Press Enter. You can make as many pages as you need to keep track of all your thoughts and ideas.

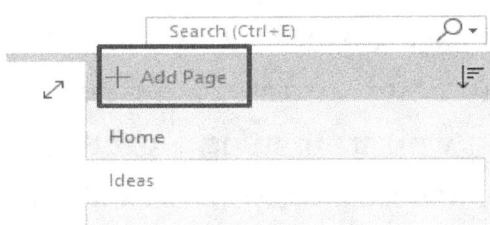

Subpages: You can make subpages inside a page to organize your information even more. With subpages, you can create hierarchies and keep information linked together. To make a subpage, right-click on an existing page and choose "New Subpage" from the menu that appears. Give the subpage a name, then press the Enter key.

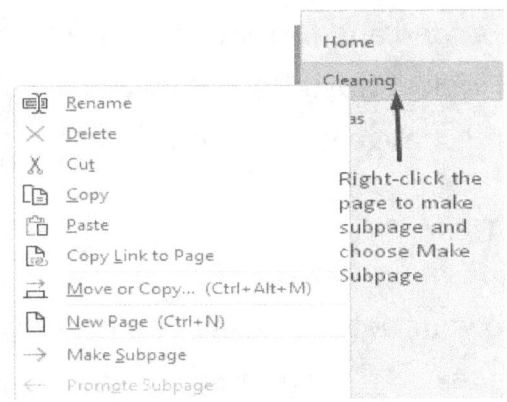

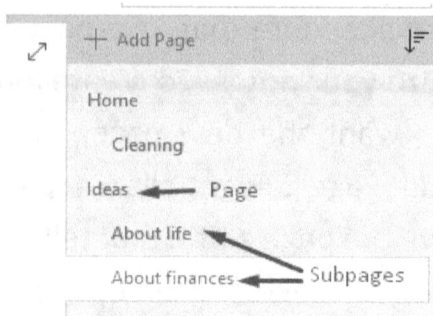

By using these ways to organize, you can keep your notes in order and make them easy to find. Whether you're a student taking notes in class, a writer coming up with ideas, or a worker putting together work-related information, Onenote gives you a flexible and easy way to keep track of your notes.

In the next part, we'll look at the different ways you can take notes and organize them in OneNote.

ADDING AND FORMATTING TEXT

Text must be added and formatted to use OneNote. In this section, we'll look at the different ways you can add text to your notes and change how it looks.

How to Add Text:

To add text to your notebook, click on the page or subpage you want the text. After choosing the place, you can start typing. OneNote has an easy-to-use design that makes adding and changing text simple. You can add text anywhere on the Page Content Area without restriction.

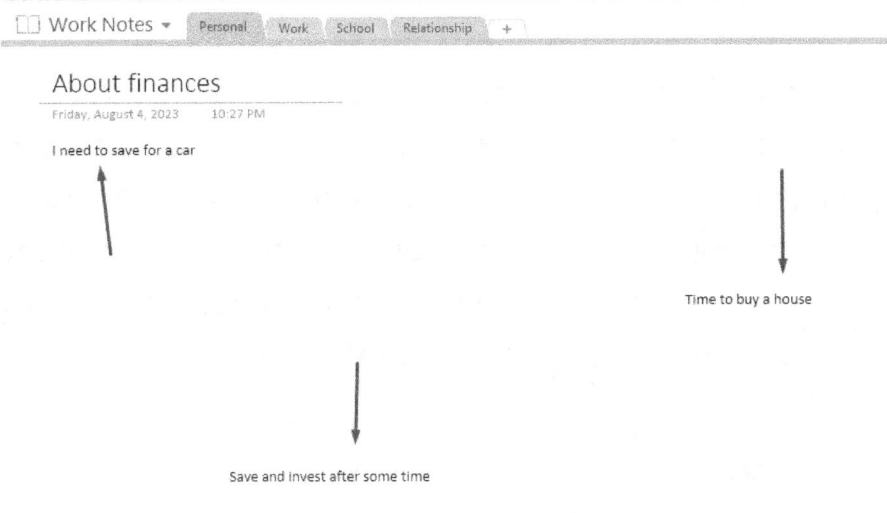

How to Format Text:

OneNote has a lot of formatting choices that let you change the way your text looks. The Home ribbon houses these formatting options. Here are some of the most important ways to organize your work:

1. Font Styles: To improve the look of your writing, you can choose from several font styles. OneNote has choices like bold, italic, underline, strikethrough, and subscript/superscript. Just highlight the words you want to change and click the right button in the toolbar.

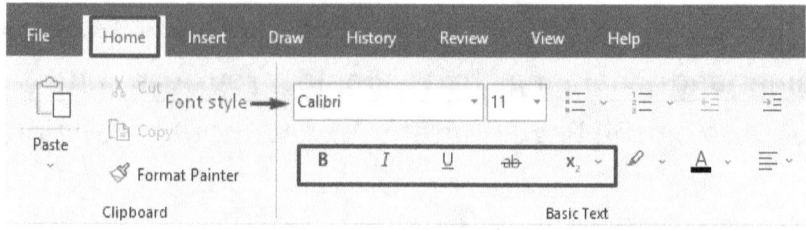

2. Font Size and Color: You can change the size and color of your text in OneNote to make it look better. You can quickly change the font size by selecting the text and using the dropdown menu in the toolbar to choose a different size. Click the "Font Color" button and choose a color from the choices to change the color of the text.

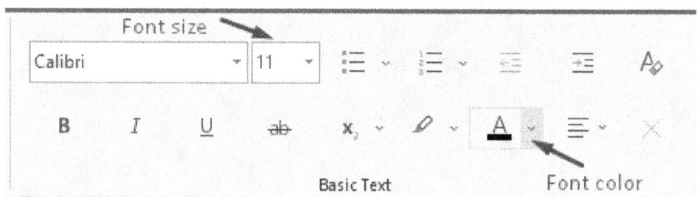

3. Text Alignment: OneNote gives you different ways to line up your text. You can put your writing on the left, right, in the middle, or justify. Choose the words you want to align and click on the button in the toolbar that says "Paragraph Alignment".

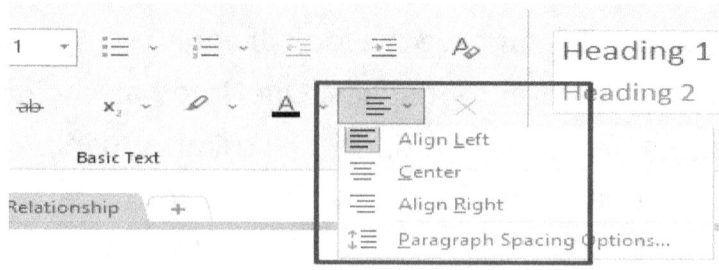

4. Bullets and numbers: To organize your information, OneNote lets you make lists with bullets or numbers. Just highlight the text and click on the "Bullets" or "Numbering" button in the toolbar. You can also change how the numbers or arrows look by choosing a different style from the dropdown menu.

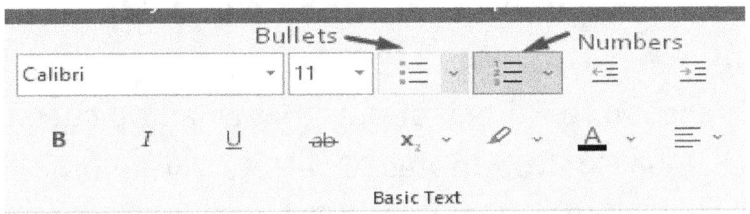

5. Indenting: There are different ways to indent your text in OneNote to make a hierarchical framework. Use the "Increase Indent" and "Decrease Indent" buttons on the toolbar to change the amount of indentation. This is very helpful when making plans or lists within lists.

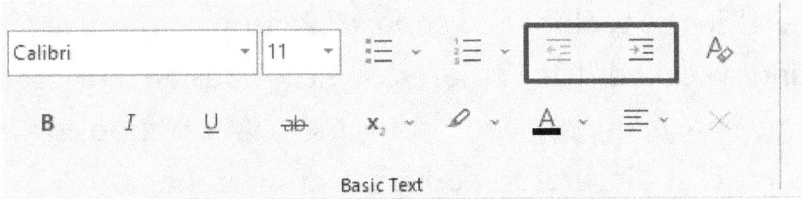

Using these text editing tools, you can make your notes look better and be more organized. OneNote has an easy-to-use interface that lets you add and style text quickly. This makes it an excellent tool for taking notes, writing, and organizing information.

In the next part, we'll look at how you can add media and attachments to your OneNote notebooks. Stay tuned for more fun and valuable OneNote features and functions for newbies.

INSERTING IMAGES AND FILES

In this section, we'll talk about how to add pictures and files to your OneNote notes. OneNote gives you a lot of ways to add visual features and files to your notes to make them more exciting and dynamic.

Adding Pictures

To add a picture to your notebook, go to the page or subpage where you want to put the image. Then, click "Insert" in the toolbar and choose "Pictures". This will open a window called "File Explorer", where you can look for the image you want on your computer. After choosing the picture, click "Insert" to add it to your notebook.

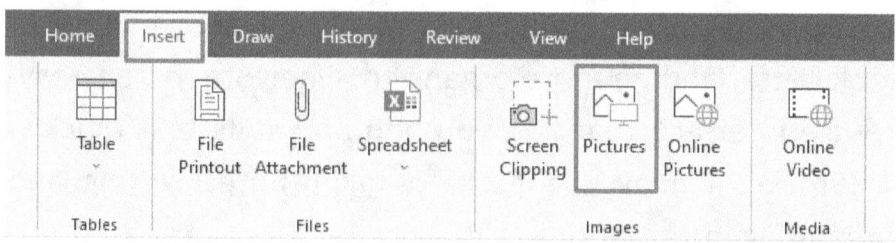

OneNote also lets you take pictures from a camera or printer right into the program. To do this, click on the "Insert" tab, choose "Pictures," and then click either "From Camera" or "From Scanner". This tool is great for quickly scanning important documents or handwritten notes.

After adding a picture to a note, OneNote lets you change its size and position. Just click on the picture to choose it, and then use the buttons to change its size. You can also move the picture around on the page by dragging it. OneNote also gives you choices for aligning the image with other things on the page.

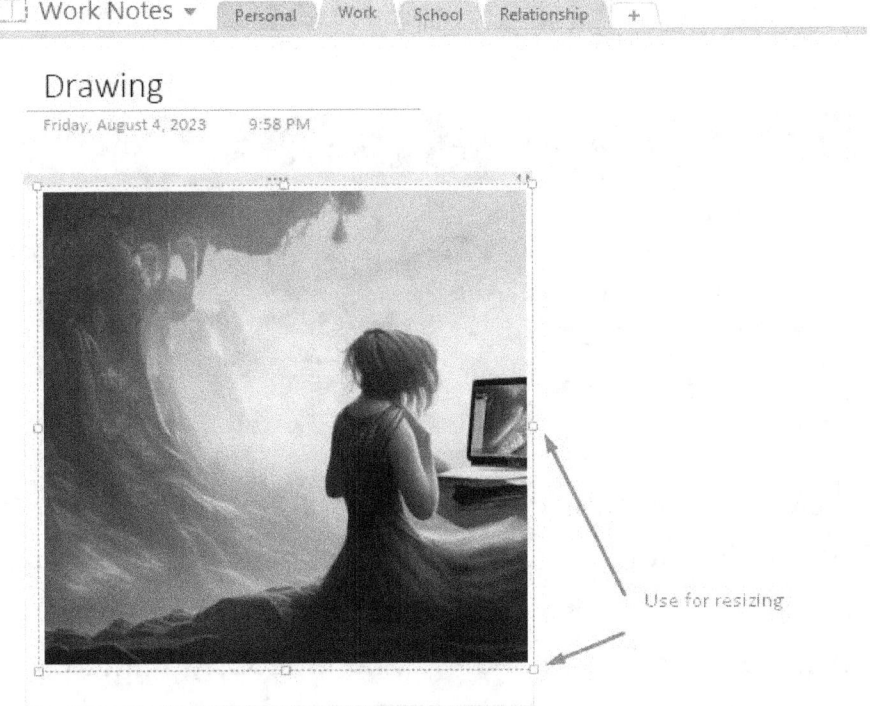

Adding Screen Clips

With this tool, you can take a picture of your screen. When working on your computer, you often find bits of information that could be useful in the future. These bits of information can be anything from a pop-up message to a web page or even breaking news, among other things. With your OneNote app, you can take a copy of this information and save it until you need it.

Open the information you want to save and arrange it so that it is easy to see on your computer screen. Open OneNote and click the "Insert" tab. Then, in the "Images" group, click "Screen Clipping".

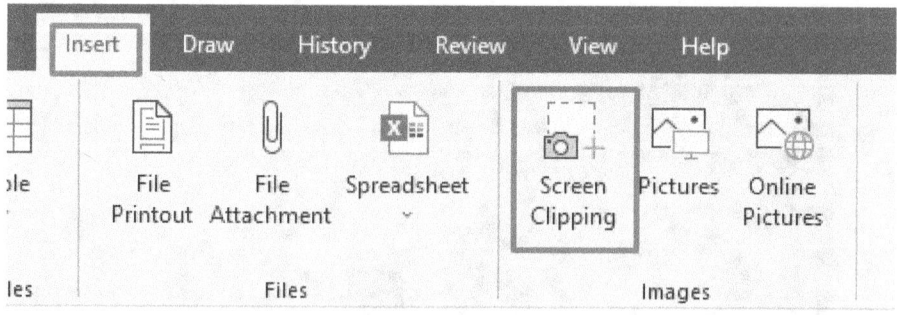

OneNote then shrinks down and takes you back to the information you already set up to be saved. Now, make your screen clip. Finally, your screenshot shows up as an image on your note and is simultaneously immediately copied to the window's clipboard.

You can also use the picture on another page of your note or in a different app. You can do this by hitting Ctrl + V on your keyboard to paste your screenshot on another page of your note or in any other app.

Putting Files in

OneNote lets you add more than just pictures to your notes. You can also add different types of files. With this feature, you can keep all necessary documents, spreadsheets, presentations, or any other file in your notes so that they are easy to find and use.

To add a file, go to the "Insert" tab on the toolbar and choose the "File Attachment" choice. This will bring up a box where you can find and select the file you want. Click "Insert" once you've picked the file to add it to your notebook. OneNote will show you a picture of the file, which you can click on to open it right from your notes.

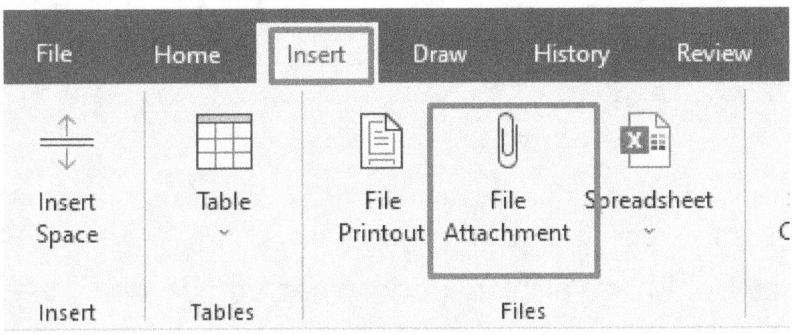

Like with images, OneNote lets you change the size and arrangement of files you add to your notes. You can also change the file's name in OneNote to make it easier to find and organize.

Sketching Shape

OneNote lets you sketch, and you can even make shapes by hand. To draw, you need to click on the "Draw" tab. You'll find everything you need to draw here.

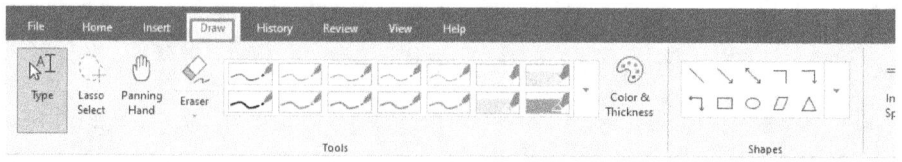

In the Tools group, choose a drawing pen. Then, in the Tools group, click "Color & Thickness" to pick a color and width for your sketch.

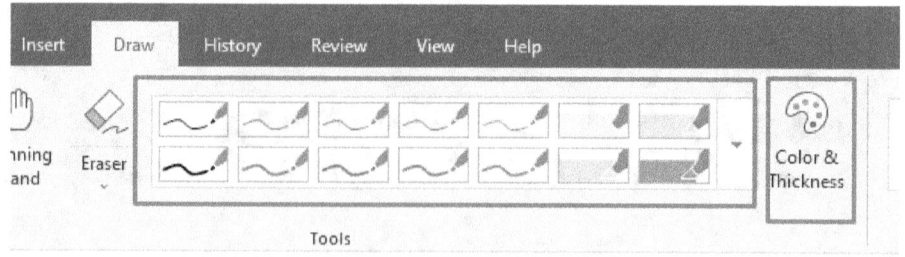

Then you can use your mouse or a pen to draw. And remember that you can undo what you've done as you draw by hitting Ctrl + Z on your keyboard if you made a mistake. When you're done drawing, click the "Type" button in the Draw ribbon to switch back to the type mode.

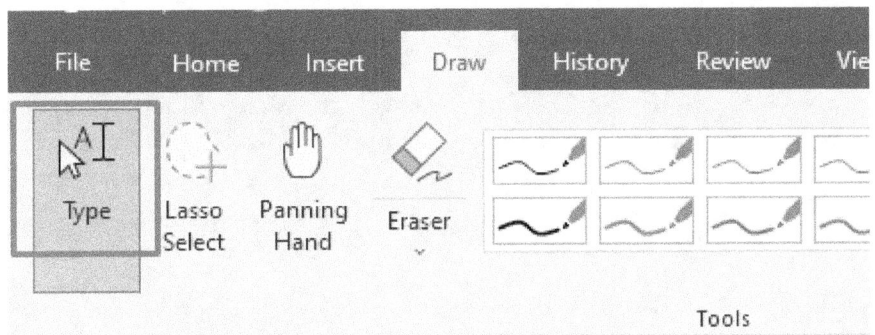

Drawing Shapes

You can draw many different kinds of shapes, from ovals to rectangles to straight lines. You are free to draw whatever you want. What is drawn is mainly based on what is needed and what is known. Because of this, you need both basic technical understanding and practice.

Choose a shape from the "Shapes" group in the "Draw" tab. Your mouse should now show a plus sign. Click and draw the shape where you want it.

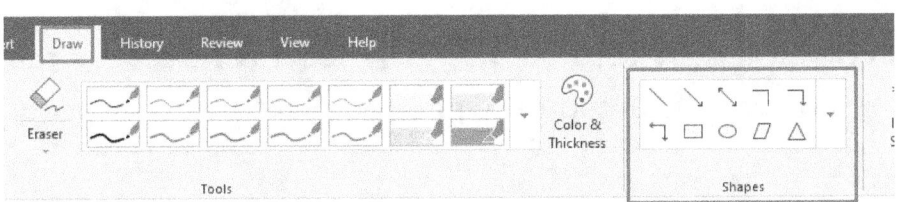

You can right-click on a shape and then choose Pen Properties to change its color and thickness.

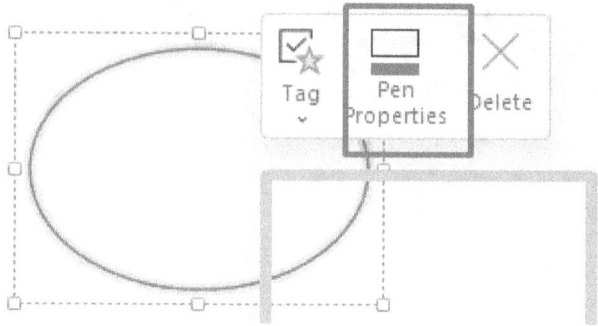

If you want to get good at drawing, you need to keep working and learn from artists who are already good. You will make a lot of mistakes, but you can always use the Undo button or Ctrl + Z to undo what you did.

Recordings of Audio and Video

Here's something else that makes your OneNote app stand out. You can add audio and video files to your work with this program. You could express yourself better and in a unique way with this function.

Click either "Record Audio" or "Record Video" in the "Insert" ribbon based on what you want to add to your note.

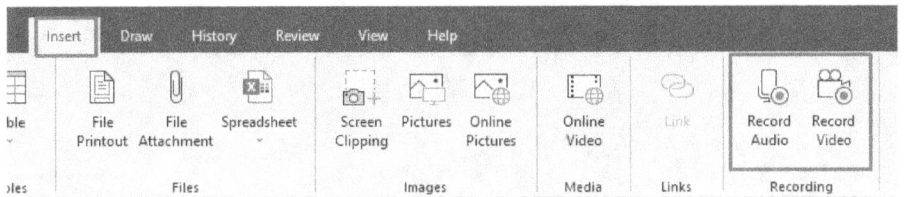

Then, a new tab called "Recording Tab" appears. This tab has all the tools you need to record, such as "play," "pause," "stop," "rewind," "fast forward," and "counter." The counter counts up as you record. When you're done, press "Stop", and the recording will go right into your note.

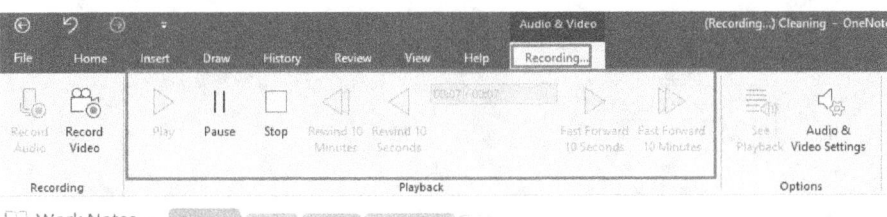

Hyperlinks

Hyperlinks are links to other sources of information that aren't directly related to your content. Your readers can click on these links to learn more about the information. This makes your material less bulky and makes people more likely to read it all. OneNote can add hyperlinks to both text and images.

Highlight the text you want to link if it has already been typed, or click once on the picture you want to link. Click "Link" in the "Insert" ribbon.

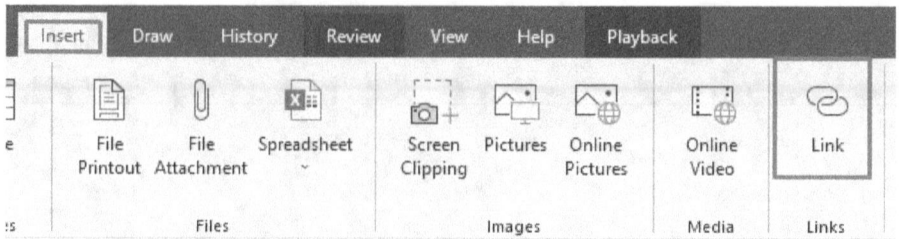

A window pops up. In the address box, type the URL of the site you want to link to your text or picture, then click OK to make it happen.

Link ✕

Text to display:

I need to save for a car

Address:

http://www.google.com/

Or pick a location in OneNote:

Search by text in title

All Notebooks

⊟ My First Notebook

⊞ Quick Notes

⊞ Private

⊞ Work

⊟ My Career

⊞ School

⊞ Work

fff

OK   Cancel

You can now click on the text or picture, and you will be taken to the page you entered. Before you click on the picture to go to the linked website, press the "Ctrl" key on your computer.

We have yet to tell you everything you need to know about hyperlinks. You still need to know how to change a hyperlink or delete it from your content. Right-click on the text or picture that is already linked and click "Edit Link" to change or remove the link. Click "Remove Link" instead to remove the link for good.

Wiki-Links

Another great thing about the OneNote app is that it has wiki-links, which let a lot of information be shared and saved from one end to the other. You can quickly connect notes from different parts of the OneNote app. You can also link your notes to the web and Office documents.

Put your cursor where you want your wiki-link, and then type [[The name of the page you want to link to]] in the style shown. Let's say you want to go to the Ideas page. You would then type something like [[Ideas]]. Now you have a wiki-link. When you click on it, you are redirected to the Ideas page.

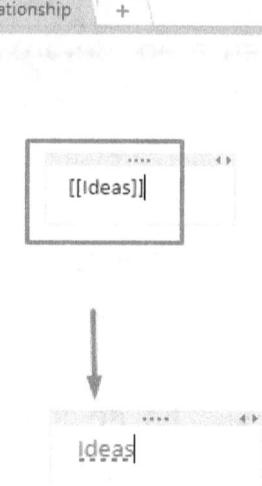

Put your cursor next to the first wiki-link you just made to make more. Press the Tab key on your computer. This will create a table. Type the name of your second wiki-link into the table's empty cell using the double bracket method shown above. For example, if you type [[Home]], the link will take you to the Home page.

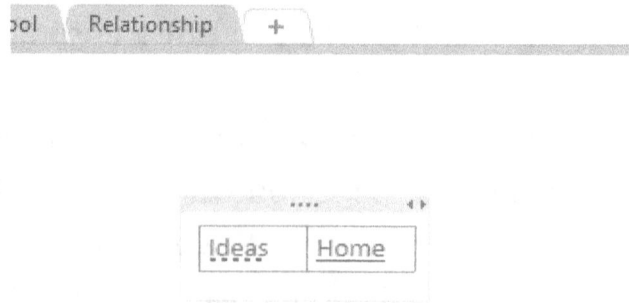

By using OneNote's ability to add images and files, you can make visually appealing notes full of all the necessary multimedia elements and links. OneNote is an excellent choice for organizing and showing information well because it is easy to use and has many different tools.

In the next section, we'll talk about how to use sections and pages to organize your notes in OneNote. Stay tuned for more fun features and ways to use OneNote that will help you get the hang of it.

ORGANIZING NOTES WITH SECTIONS AND PAGES

In this part, we'll talk more about how to use sections and pages to organize your notes in OneNote. Sections and pages are important parts of OneNote that let you organize your notes in a way that makes sense.

Sections:

Your notes are kept in sections in OneNote. They act as broad categories that group similar contents. Sections are like folders in a standard filing system. By making sections, you can quickly divide your notebooks into sections for different topics, projects, or subjects.

To add a new section, click the "+" button in the sidebar next to a current section. This will open a new tab for your section, where you can give it a name and change how it looks.

You can choose a different color for each section to make it easy to find your way around by right-clicking on the section and selecting "Section Color".

You can start adding pages to a section once you've created it. Pages are where you write your notes and keep them. Each section can have more than one page, which makes it easy to arrange and find your content by topic or subtopic.

Pages:

Pages in OneNote are like blank boards where you can write down your thoughts, ideas, and information. They are the separate parts of your notes that let you make different documents for different goals or topics.

To add a new page, just click the "+" button next to the pages within a section. This will bring up a fresh page where you can start writing or typing your notes. You can also add pictures, tables, music files, and other multimedia to your notes to make them more exciting and valuable.

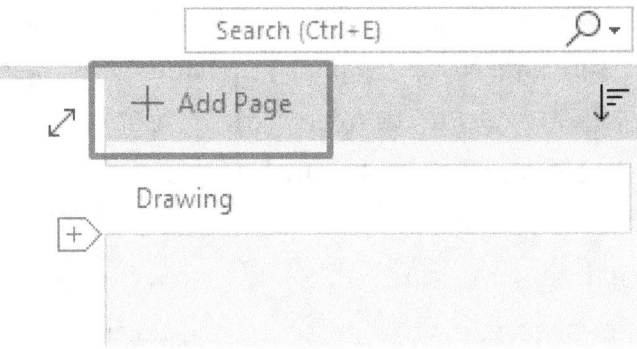

On each page, you can organize your notes in any way you want. You can arrange your content and make a clear hierarchy with headings, bullet points, numbering, and other formatting tools. This makes it easier to scan your notes and find what you want quickly.

To move between sections and pages, click on the tabs in the sidebar that say "section" or "page". This makes it easy for you to move between different sections and pages, making it easy to take notes.

You can make a complete and well-organized system for your notes in OneNote by using sections and pages well. You can divide your content into sections based on different projects or themes, and pages give you a place to write and store your notes. Whether you are a student, a worker, or just someone who likes to write things down, learning to organize your notes with sections and pages will make you much more productive and efficient.

In the next section, we'll examine simple math problems in OneNote. Stay tuned for more fun features and ways to use OneNote that will help you get the hang of it.

SIMPLE MATH CALCULATIONS

Even after you've used this friendly program extensively, you'll be amazed by its additional features. Using formulae to execute even elementary arithmetic and logic tasks is one of these truly incredible features.

First, click the area on the page where you'd like to do the math calculation. Enter the numeric expression that you want to calculate. To receive your answer, type = followed by the Enter key on your keyboard.

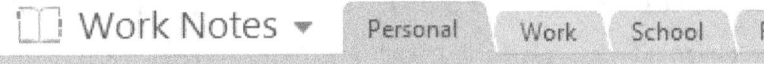
About finances

Friday, August 4, 2023   10:27 PM

I need to save for a car

Time to buy a house

Save and invest after some time

> .... ◄ ►
>
> 900 + 750 = 1,650|

To adjust the equation, click on it and enter the new numbers. While using the OneNote app to perform operations like (12 + 16) + (65 - 40), you must understand that the software follows the sequence of precedence as specified by BODMAS (Bracket Off Division Multiplication Add Subtraction). If the calculation above is performed using the OneNote app, the result is fifty-three (53).

> .... ◄ ►
>
> 900 + 750 = 1,650
>
> (12 + 16) + (65 - 40) = 53

In the next chapter, we'll look at different ways to manage your notebooks. Stay tuned for more fun features and ways to use OneNote that will help you get the hang of it.

CHAPTER 3 → MANAGING YOUR NOTEBOOKS

Now that you can create and organize notebooks, let's look into various ways to manage notebooks.

HOW TO SAVE NOTEBOOKS

OneNote automatically saves your work. If you are signed in to OneNote with a Microsoft account and connected to the internet, your notebooks are instantly saved to the cloud (OneDrive). OneNote syncs your changes regularly so that your notes are always up to date on all your devices.

Overall, the automatic saving and syncing features of OneNote give you peace of mind that your notes are safe and can be accessed on all your devices. In addition, creating manual backups of your important notes will give you even more peace of mind.

EXPORTING NOTEBOOKS

You can make a backup of your notes or share them with people who don't have access to your OneNote account by exporting notebooks. OneNote gives you different ways to export, depending on what you need. Here's how you can export your notebooks:

Exporting an Entire Notebook:

Open the OneNote app and open the notebook you want to export. Click on the "File" tab and choose "Export".

How to Export a Section:

Open the OneNote app and open the notebook with the section you want to export. Right-click on the section you wish to export in the list of sections. Choose "Export".

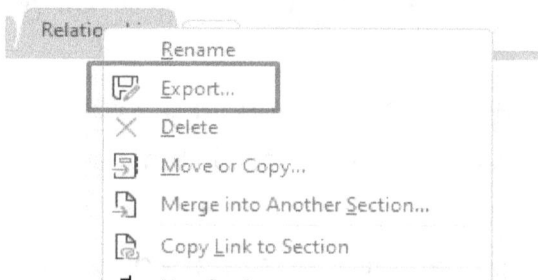

Choose the format to export:

After you click "Export", you'll be asked to choose a file format for the export.

OneNote Package (*.one): This format keeps the full notebook or section, including all pages, attachments, and formatting. It can be used to share your whole notebook or back it up.

PDF (*.pdf): This format exports the chosen notebook or section as a PDF file, which can be used to share or print your notes in a static format.

Word Document (*.docx): This format exports the chosen notebook or section as a Word document, turning your notes into a Word file with editable text.

Single File Web Page (*.mht): This format saves the chosen notebook or section as a single file with embedded images and formatting that can be viewed offline in a web browser.

Choose Destination:

After choosing the export format, you can select where you want the exported file to be saved. You can give the saved file a name.

Finish the Export:

To finish the export process, click the "Save" or "Export" button. OneNote will put the saved file in the folder you choose and in the format you chose.

Once you've downloaded a file, you can share it with others or save it as a backup on your computer or an external drive. Remember that exporting saves a snapshot of your notes at that moment; any changes you make to the source notebook after exporting won't appear in the exported file. If you want to ensure your backups are always up-to-date, you can regularly share your notes or use OneNote's automatic sync with OneDrive. This will ensure that your notes are always backed up in real-time.

SETTING A PASSWORD TO PROTECT YOUR NOTE

This function keeps other people from getting into certain parts of your notes. There may be parts of your note, like personal sections of your notes, that you don't want the person or people you're sharing it with to see. If you put a password on these sections, your recipient(s) won't be able to see them.

Right-click on the section you want to protect with a password and choose "Password Protect This Section." A password security window appears on the right side of your computer screen. Click "Set Password" to create a password.

In the Enter Password and Confirm Password boxes, type the password you want to use. It should be something easy to remember. In the password security pane, click "Lock All". This locks the section right away.

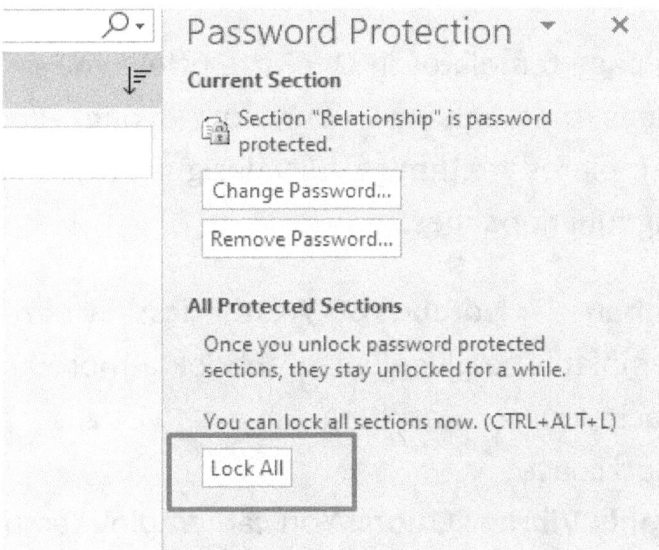

Now that you have locked the area, you may need help getting into the locked sections of your notebook. Click anywhere on the locked area and type in the password you already set.

To get rid of a password or change it:

Right-click the section and choose "Password Protect This Section". You should see "Change Password" and "Remove Password" on the password security pane. To get rid of your password, click "Remove Password". Type in the current password and click OK. Click the "X" at the top right of the password security pane to close it.

USING PAGE TEMPLATES

Utilizing page templates in OneNote offers you a range of advantages that enhance your note-taking experience. These templates are thoughtfully designed to facilitate the following functionalities:

1. **Enhance Notebook Aesthetics:** Utilize page templates to give your notebook a more appealing background, resulting in a visually pleasing workspace.
2. **Apply Vibrant Colors:** You can employ templates to infuse vibrant colors into your notebook's pages, adding a touch of creativity and distinction.
3. **Establish Consistency and Uniformity:** Page templates enable you to establish a cohesive and

consistent layout across your notebook, providing a unified appearance to your content.

To use these templates, click on the "Insert" tab and then select "Page Templates." The template pane will appear on the right side of your screen. To reveal more options within each template category, click the small arrows adjacent to the category labels.

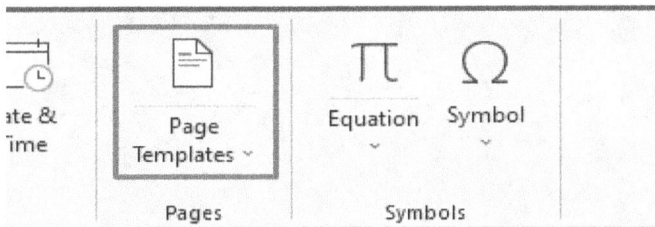

It's important to note that OneNote boasts an array of templates that cater to diverse aspects of life. Each template selection generates a separate new page automatically.

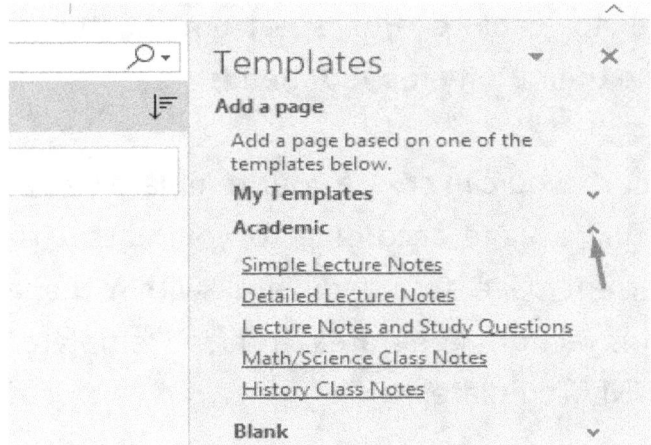

Choose the specific section in which you want to apply the template. Click on the desired template, prompting the creation of a new page tailored to the template's structure.

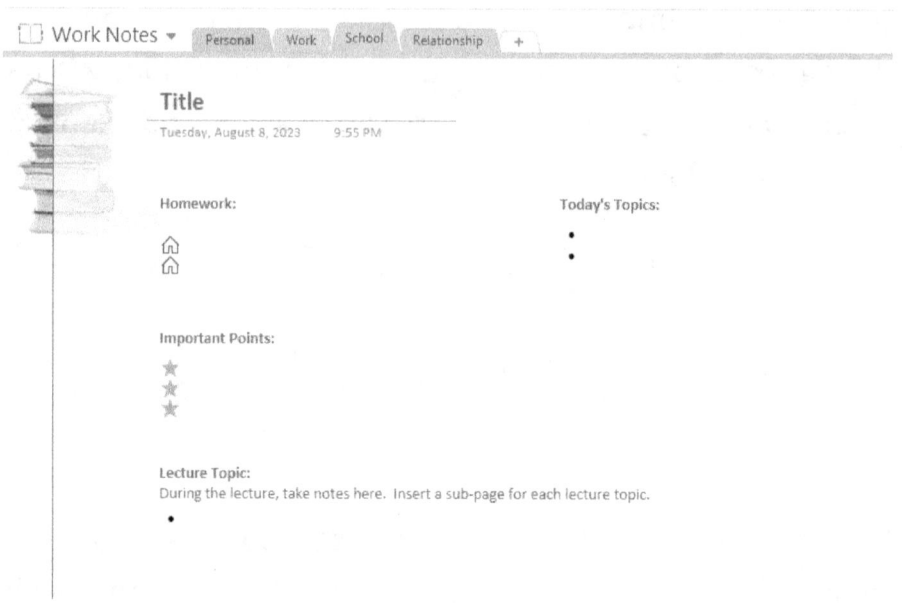

If you accidentally select an undesired template, opt for a different one and delete the initially generated page. Take the time to explore the spectrum of templates to determine their utility for your needs.

Furthermore, you can create your template by developing and crafting a page according to your taste. Then click "Save current page as a template" within the template pane. This action generates a new template section labelled "My Templates."

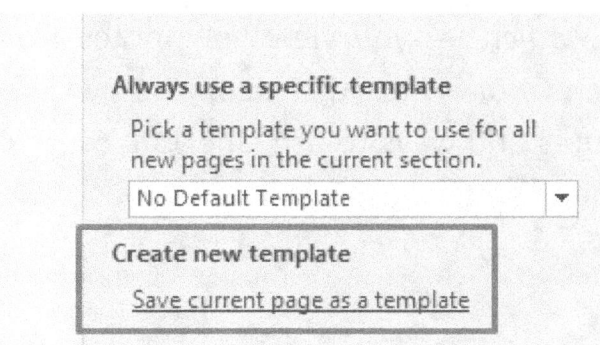

Whenever you want to use your self-made templates, select "My Templates" in the template plane to access and apply them as needed.

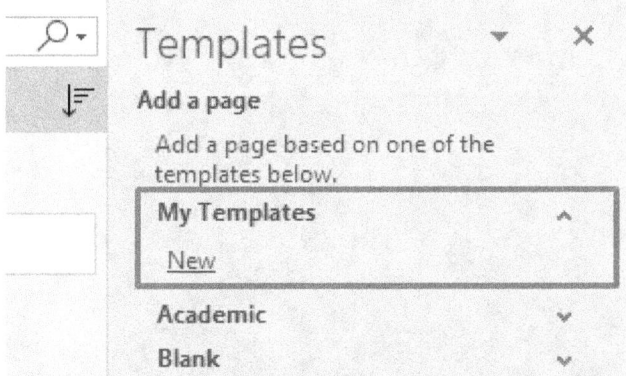

By harnessing the potential of page templates in OneNote, you can optimize your notebooks' aesthetic appeal and organizational structure, enhancing the overall note-taking experience.

In the next chapter, we'll look at how to collaborate with others seamlessly and OneNote's synchronization features, which let you view your notes from different devices and work with other people. Stay tuned for more fun features and ways to use OneNote that will help you get the hang of it.

CHAPTER 4 → COLLABORATING AND SHARING

Now that you know how to manage notebooks, let's discuss how to work with others and share notebooks in OneNote.

Collaboration is a crucial part of using OneNote, especially for people who work in teams or need to share their notes with others. In this section, we'll look at some helpful tips and methods for getting the most out of OneNote's collaboration features.

You can quickly share your notebooks with others using OneNote, which makes it easy to work together. To share a notebook, click on the "File" tab and choose "Share" *(You will need to put your notebook on OneDrive or SharePoint to be able to share)*. Then you can type in the email names of the people you want to have access to the notebook. They will get an invite to view the notebook and work together on it.

SHARING NOTEBOOKS WITH OTHERS

Sharing notebooks with others is an essential aspect of OneNote that lets people work on projects together or share information with coworkers, friends, or family. In this section, we'll discuss how to share your notes with others.

1. Sharing a notebook with certain people:

- With OneNote, you can share a notebook with specific people by sending them an email invitation. This is an excellent choice if you want to work on a project or task with a small group of people. You can easily decide how much access each person has to the notebook, whether they can look at it, edit it, or add to it.

2. Send a link to a notebook:

- You can make a sharing link for your notebook if you want to show it to more people or let anyone with the link see it. This is an easy way to share information or tools with a large group, like a class or a team. You can choose whether the link only lets people see the notebook or also lets them change it.

3. Use a public network or the cloud to share a notebook:

- You can also share your notebooks on a shared network or cloud storage tool, like Microsoft SharePoint or OneDrive. This is a good choice if you work for a company or on a team that uses these platforms to share information and work together. It ensures that everyone can work simultaneously on the most up-to-date version of the notebook.

4. Working together in real-time:

- Working together in real-time is one of the best things about sharing notes with others. This means that more than one person can make changes, add information, or leave comments on the same notebook at the same time. It makes teams working on the same project or goal more productive and more accessible for them to work together.

5. Changes on more than one device:

- When you share a notebook, OneNote syncs your changes across all your devices. This means you can get to your notebook and work on it from any device, like your computer, tablet, or phone. It lets you stay in touch and get things done even when you're on the move.

In this section, we discussed the different ways you can share your OneNote notes with others. Using these sharing features, you can improve collaboration, simplify communication, and make your process more efficient. OneNote gives you the tools you need to share and work together on your notebooks, whether working on a personal project, working with a team, or sharing information with a bigger audience. So, go ahead and tell the world what you know and think.

COLLABORATING ON SHARED NOTEBOOKS

One of the best things about sharing notes in OneNote is that you can work together in real-time. This means that more than one person can make changes, add information, or leave comments on the same notebook at the same time. In this section, we'll talk about the different ways you can work together on shared notes in OneNote.

1. Editing in real-time:

- Everyone can make real-time changes when working together on a shared notebook. This means that when one person makes a change, others will immediately see it. Real-time writing makes it easy for everyone to work together on a group project, do research, or take meeting notes. It also makes sure that everyone is on the same page.

2. Commenting and feedback:

- OneNote also has a commenting tool that lets users leave feedback or ideas on specific pages or sections of a shared notebook. This is especially helpful when different people are working on different parts of a project and need to talk about their ideas or thoughts. Comments are easy to read and respond to, which helps people work together and encourages open communication.

3. Changes over time:

- OneNote has a tool called "Version History" that lets users see and go back to older versions of a shared notebook if there are any conflicts or differences. This ensures no data or changes are lost and gives a safety net in case someone makes a mistake or deletes important information by accident. The version history feature makes it easy to work together without worrying about making mistakes that can't be fixed.

4. Setting goals and tasks:

- Users can use OneNote to put tasks and due dates in a shared notebook. This is especially helpful for groups or teams working on projects with multiple goals or milestones. Team members can easily see what needs to be done, who is in charge of each job, and when it needs to be done. This makes it easier to keep track of what everyone is doing and ensure that all project requirements are met on time.

5. Messages and alerts:

- OneNote has alert and notification features to keep everyone engaged and up to date. Users can choose to be notified when changes are made to a shared notebook or when notes are added. This ensures that everyone is up-to-date and can reply quickly to any changes or conversations in the notebook. Notifications and alerts help keep people working together and keep the project from getting behind schedule.

By using OneNote's collaboration features, you can improve teamwork, boost productivity, and make your process more efficient. OneNote gives you the tools you need to work well with others on shared notes, whether working on a group project, doing research, or just sharing ideas. So, start working together right away and use OneNote to its fullest for projects with your team or on your own.

SYNCING AND ACCESSING NOTEBOOKS ACROSS DEVICES

Syncing notebooks across devices:

- One of the best things about OneNote is that you can sync your notes on all your devices. This means you can access your notes and material from your computer, tablet, or phone. This ensures you always have all the vital information you need at your fingertips, no matter where you are. Whether at the office, on the go, or working from home, OneNote keeps all of your devices' notes in sync and up to date.

- To sync your notebooks, sign in to your Microsoft account on each device you want to use to view your notebooks. Once you're signed in, any changes or additions you make on one device will instantly show up on all your other devices. This seamless syncing ensures you never miss a beat and can always see the latest version of your notes, no matter what device you're using.

- Syncing also makes it easy to work with other people. If you and your coworkers or partners are working on the same notebook, syncing ensures that everyone has the most up-to-date version. This removes the need to send files back and forth or worry about different versions of the same paper. With the sharing features of OneNote, everyone can stay on the same page and work well together.

Accessing notebooks offline:

- Another benefit of OneNote is that you can view your notebooks even when you're not online. This is especially helpful when you're on an airplane or working in a remote area where you don't have access to the internet.

- To use your notebooks when you're not online, save them to your computer. This lets you see and change your notes even when you're not connected to the internet. When you get back online, any changes you made when you weren't connected will automatically sync to the cloud. This way, your notes will always be up to date.

- You can also choose which notebooks to download so you can view them when you're not online. You can put the notebooks you need most at the top of the list while saving memory space on your device. Since you can access your notebooks even when you're not online, you can work on your projects and take notes no matter where you are. This makes OneNote a convenient and helpful tool.

In the next section, we'll look at how to collaborate with others seamlessly. Keep an eye out for more cool tips and tricks!

CHAPTER 5 → TIPS AND TRICKS

Here are some tips and tricks to help you make the most of OneNote and improve your note-taking and organization experience.

TIME-SAVING SHORTCUTS

To use OneNote well, you must know how to use computer shortcuts. This part will focus on shortcuts and keyboard actions that will save you time, help you work faster, and take better notes.

1. Shortcuts for navigating:

- Press Ctrl and Home to go to the top of the page.

- Ctrl + End: Go to the page's end.

- Press Ctrl and the up arrow to move up the page.

- Press Ctrl and the down arrow to move down the page.

- Press Ctrl + Page Up to go back a page.

- Ctrl + Page Down: Move to the next page.

2. Shortcuts for formatting:

- Press Ctrl + B to make the chosen text bold.

- Press Ctrl + I to make a piece of text bold.

- Press Ctrl + U to highlight the words.

- Press Ctrl + Alt + > to make the font bigger.

- Press Ctrl + Shift + to make the font size smaller.

3. Shortcuts for editing:

- Ctrl + X: Cuts the text or item you have chosen.

- Ctrl+C: Copies the text or object you have chosen.

- Ctrl+V: Paste text or an object that has been cut or copied.

- Ctrl+Z: Undo the last thing you did.

- Ctrl+Y: Undo the last thing you did.

- Press Ctrl+F to look for text on the current page.

4. Shortcuts for Organizing:

- Press Ctrl + Alt + N to start a new page.

- Press Ctrl, Alt, Shift, and N to start a new part.

- Press Ctrl + Alt + M to start a new notebook.

- Press Ctrl + Shift + L to make a new note folder.

- Press Ctrl + Shift + E to make a note container bigger or smaller.

5. Shortcuts for Working Together:

- Press Ctrl + Shift + S to share the page you're on.

- Press Ctrl + Shift + C to copy a link to the current page.

- Press Ctrl + Shift + D to email the page you're on.

- Press Ctrl + Shift + P to print the page you're on.

Remember that using these shortcuts often will help you learn how to use OneNote well, saving you time and effort. By understanding these keyboard commands, you can explore, format, edit, organize, and work together on your notes more effectively.

TRANSFORMING IMAGES TO TEXT

Have you ever encountered an image that captivated you with its text, only to find yourself labouring to type out the content—regardless of its length—wasting valuable time that could have been better invested in more productive pursuits? With the aid of your OneNote app, this entire process can now be completed in a fraction of a second, thanks to the Optical Character Recognition (OCR) feature.

To transform an image into text, integrate the image containing the desired text into your note. As we've previously explored screen clips and image insertion, you're well-versed in this aspect.

Right-click the image and opt for the "Copy Text from Picture" choice. Conclude the process by right-clicking any available space on your screen and selecting "Paste." Witness the extracted text content unfold before your eyes.

But wait, there's more! You can also search for text within an image. Following uploading the image housing the text, go to the search bar and type in the content you're seeking. Observe as OneNote skillfully highlights your search results in real-time as you type.

Experience the ease and efficiency of converting images into text through OneNote's Optical Character Recognition (OCR) capability, sparing you the drudgery of manual transcription and ushering in newfound productivity.

USING ONENOTE WITH MICROSOFT OUTLOOK

In this section, we'll talk about how OneNote and Microsoft Outlook work together and how you can use these two vital tools together to stay more organized.

1. Adding pages from OneNote to Outlook:

One of the best things about OneNote is that you can link notes to other programs, like Outlook. You can easily link a note in OneNote to a job, meeting, or email in Outlook.

- To do this, open the note you want to link in OneNote, right-click on the page, and choose "Copy Link to Page."

- Next, open Microsoft Outlook and go to the job, meeting, or email you want to link to the OneNote page.

- Right-click on the task, meeting, or email and choose "Paste Link." This will add a link you can click on to go straight to the OneNote page.

2. How to Send Pages from OneNote as Emails from Outlook:

- OneNote and Outlook work well together because you can send OneNote pages as emails straight from OneNote.

- To do this, open the note in OneNote that you want to send as an email.

- In the top left part of the OneNote window, click on the "File" tab.

- Choose "Send" and select "Email Page" from the drop-down choice. This will make Microsoft Outlook open a new email with the OneNote page linked as a PDF file.

- After that, you can add recipients, a topic, and any other information before sending the email.

3. Adding meeting notes from OneNote to the Outlook calendar:

If you take meeting notes in OneNote, it's easy to link them to the meeting in Microsoft Outlook.

- Start the meeting in Outlook and click the "Meeting Notes" button on the ribbon to do this.

- Choose "Take Notes on Your Own" or "Shared Notes" based on your wants.

- This will start a new page for the meeting notes in OneNote. Any changes or additions to the meeting notes in OneNote will be made immediately in Outlook.

Integrating OneNote and Microsoft Outlook lets you easily handle your tasks, meetings, and emails while keeping all the essential information in OneNote. This integration gives you a complete and quick way to take notes, keep track of tasks, and talk to people. In the next section, we'll look at more tips and tricks for getting the most out of OneNote and being as productive as possible. Stay tuned for more important information!

TIPS FOR STUDENTS ON TAKING NOTES

In this part, we'll talk about different ways for students and researchers to take notes. Taking good notes is important for school success, and OneNote has many features and tools to help you take better notes. By putting these tips into their study habit, students can get the most out of their learning and do better in school.

1. Method of Cornell:

The Cornell method is a famous way to take notes that tells students to separate their notes into different parts. The organized style of OneNote makes it easy to use this method. Students can create a template with three parts: a narrow column on the left for cues or questions, a bigger column on the right for the main notes, and a section at the bottom for summarizing the most important points. This method gets people involved with the information and makes it easier to review and change it.

2. Using a mind map:

The digital canvas in OneNote is a great place to make mind maps, a visual way to take notes that help students order and link ideas. Students can easily make nodes and branches, add pictures and links, and move things around thanks to its easy-to-use interface. Mind maps are beneficial for people who learn best by seeing things. They spark imagination and help people understand complex topics better.

3. Method of Outlining:

The outline method is a simple way to take notes that emphasizes order and structure. With OneNote's bullet and numbering tools, it's easy to make clear and well-organized sketches. Students can easily indent and expand parts, which makes it easier to find their way around and understand. This is a great way to summarize lectures, textbook chapters, and research papers.

4. Notes on Images:

Because OneNote is so flexible, students can add diagrams, graphs, and pictures to their notes. Visual notes not only make learning more fun, but they also help you remember what you've learned. Students can better understand their learning and complete a study guide by putting together text and pictures.

5. Collaboration:

Collaboration tools in OneNote are beneficial for group projects and study groups. Students can make shared notes where they can work together in real-time. This lets them combine their information, share resources, and learn from different points of view. Also, the syncing features of OneNote ensure everyone has access to the latest information.

6. Tags and the ability to search:

OneNote's tagging and search features make organizing and finding notes much more accessible. Students can add terms to their notes to make it easier to find specific information in the future. Also, OneNote's powerful search tool lets students find particular words or ideas quickly across all of their notes, saving them a lot of time while studying for exams.

By adding these ways to take notes to their OneNote routine, students and teachers can make the most of their learning and improve their education as a whole. OneNote is a complete platform for taking good notes in academic settings. It can be used to organize ideas, work with peers, or review and revise materials.

ONENOTE FOR WORKERS AND MANAGING PROJECTS

In this section, we'll look at how professionals and project managers can use the power of OneNote to be more productive and handle their projects better. OneNote has many features and tools that can help streamline processes, make it easier to work together and ensure projects get done successfully.

1. Planning and organizing for a project:

OneNote is an excellent tool for planning and organizing projects because it has a clear style and lets you take notes in different ways. Professionals and project managers can make notebooks for each project. In these notebooks, they can write down the project's goals, set milestones, and break jobs down into steps that can be taken. They can use the bullet and numbering tools in OneNote to make hierarchical lists and keep track of work throughout the lifecycle of a project. Using OneNote's tagging feature, they can quickly put tasks in order of importance, set reminders, and give team members tasks.

2. Notes and Minutes from a Meeting:

OneNote is a great way to take notes and minutes at meetings. Professionals can make a different section in their project notebooks to write down what was said, what was decided, and what needs to be done after a meeting. With OneNote's ability to record audio, they can ensure that their notes are correct and complete even when meetings move quickly. Also, the tagging tool in OneNote lets them mark important points, follow up on action items, and keep track of the progress that was talked about in meetings.

3. Collaboration and working as a team:

Collaboration tools in OneNote are beneficial for workers and project managers who work in teams. They can make shared notebooks where team members can work together in real-time. This makes it easy to share updates, come up with new ideas, look over project papers and give feedback. The syncing features of OneNote ensure everyone has access to the most recent information and changes that team members have made.

4. Documentation for a project and managing its resources:

OneNote can be a central place to store project tools and documentation. Professionals and project managers can add files, images, and links to their notes, making it easy to find important documents and information. OneNote's powerful search feature makes it easy for them to see the resources they need without looking through many files and emails.

5. Integration with Tools for Getting Things Done:

OneNote works well with other productivity tools and makes it easier for workers and project managers to do their jobs. They can keep track of project progress by linking OneNote pages to tasks in project management tools like Microsoft Planner or Trello. Because OneNote works with Microsoft Outlook, they can turn emails into tasks and add them to their project notebooks.

By adding OneNote to their professional and project management workflows, professionals and project managers can better plan and carry out their projects, improve communication and teamwork within their teams, and ultimately be successful in what they do.

ONENOTE FOR CREATIVE WRITING AND PLANNING A BOOK

In this section, we'll look at how writers and other creative people can use the power of OneNote to improve their writing, organize their ideas, and plan their books or stories well. OneNote has many features and tools that can help writers manage their work, develop new ideas, and bring their creative thoughts to life.

1. Coming up with ideas and brainstorming:

OneNote gives writers a blank page where they can write down ideas, random thoughts, and motivation. With its flexible note-taking features, writers can make sections or pages for different parts of their story, like characters, plotlines, places, or themes. They can use OneNote's "digital ink" feature to draw pictures or mind maps to connect thoughts and look into different options.

2. Character growth and worldbuilding:

In creative writing, it's important to make interesting characters and places that pull the reader in. With OneNote, writers can make detailed character profiles that include the character's appearance, personality, past, and reasons for doing what they do. They can create different sections or pages for each character, which lets them go into more detail about who they are and how they relate to each other. In the same way, writers can use OneNote to make detailed notes about the settings, rules, events, and cultures of the worlds they are making up.

3. Plan and Storyboard:

OneNote is an excellent tool for planning and outlining a book or story because of how it is set up. Writers can make notebooks or sections to outline the general plot, each chapter, or a particular scene. They can use the bullet and numbering tools in OneNote to organize their thoughts in a hierarchical way that makes sense. Using the tags feature in OneNote, writers can mark important plot points, keep track of how their story is going, and quickly move around in their outlines.

4. Research and Management of References:

When people write creatively, they often do a lot of studies to add depth and realism to their stories. Writers can use OneNote to keep all their study materials in one place, like articles, images, websites, or interviews. Writers can add files or links to their notes, making it easy to find helpful information while writing. OneNote's vital search feature makes it easy for writers to find specific references quickly, so they don't have to look through piles of paper or digital documents.

5. Work Together and Get Feedback:

Writers who work in groups or want feedback from beta readers or editors can use OneNote's tools that help people work together. Writers can make shared notebooks where they can work together in real-time, share their work, and get comments or ideas. The synchronization features of OneNote ensure that everyone has access to the most recent version of the text or notes.

By using OneNote as part of their creative writing process, writers can make their work easier, better organize their ideas, and bring their stories to life. OneNote is an excellent tool for writers because it can be used in many different ways and has many other features. This helps writers be more creative and write more interesting stories.

ONENOTE FOR PERSONAL ORGANIZATION AND GOAL TRACKING

In this section, we'll look at how to use OneNote to organize your life and keep track of your goals. OneNote is a robust tool not only for writers and other creative people but also for people who want to stay organized, keep track of their tasks, and keep their goals in mind.

1. Getting things done:

OneNote has many features that help people stay on top of their chores. Users can make to-do lists, set reminders, and, if they are working as a team, give tasks to particular people. The tagging tool in OneNote makes it easy for users to sort their tasks by priority, due date, or status. They can also use checkboxes to mark jobs as done, which gives them a good feeling of having done something.

2. Planning each day and keeping track of time:

OneNote can be a digital calendar, letting users plan their days, weeks, or months. They can make sections or pages for each day where they can write down their plans, meetings, and important dates. OneNote is flexible, so users can quickly add and move tasks around. This makes sure that time is used well and efficiently.

3. Setting and following goals:

Setting goals is an essential part of growing and developing as a person. OneNote lets users set short-term and long-term goals and track how they're doing. Users can make parts or pages for each goal and write down the steps they need to take to reach it. They can keep track of their progress and stay encouraged by using the checkboxes or progress bars in OneNote.

4. Tracking habits:

Getting good habits is the key to being successful in life. OneNote can be used to keep track of people's daily habits and make them answer for what they do. Users can create tables or checklists to keep track of habits like working out, reading, meditating, or learning a skill. They can look over their habit tracking records often to find patterns, stay inspired, and make any needed changes.

5. Keeping a personal journal:

OneNote can be used as a digital journal where people can write down their ideas, feelings, and thoughts. Users can make parts or pages for different topics or periods, which makes it easy to move around in their journals. OneNote's multimedia features let users add photos, audio recordings, or even video clips to their journal notes, making a personal archive that is rich and immersive.

6. Planning money and keeping track of expenses:

OneNote can be used for budgeting and keeping track of expenses. Users can make their pages or sections to handle their budgets, keep track of their spending, and keep an eye on their financial goals. With OneNote's ability to attach files and links, users can keep all their financial papers, like bills and receipts, in one place, making it easy to find them when needed.

By using OneNote to keep track of their tasks and goals, people can stay on top of their work, handle their time well, and work toward achieving their goals. OneNote is an excellent tool for personal growth because it is flexible and easy to use. It helps people stay organized and inspired in their daily lives.

EXERCISES

Certainly! Here are some exercises designed for beginners to get familiar with using Microsoft OneNote:

Exercise 1: Creating Your First Notebook

1. Open OneNote and sign in with your Microsoft account.
2. Click on "File" in the top-left corner and choose "New Notebook."
3. Give your notebook a name and select a location to save it (OneDrive or your local device).
4. Click "Create" to finish creating your notebook.

Exercise 2: Organizing Sections and Pages

1. Inside your newly created notebook, click "New Section" to create a section.
2. Rename the section to something relevant, like "Personal," "Work," or "School."
3. Create a new page within the section by clicking on "+ Page" or right-clicking the section and choosing "New Page."
4. Give the page a title and add some text or content.

Exercise 3: Formatting Text and Adding Images

1. On the page you created, type some text.
2. Experiment with text formatting options such as bold, italics, underline, font styles, and colors.
3. Insert an image by clicking "Insert" in the top menu and selecting "Pictures."
4. Resize and reposition the image within your page.

Exercise 4: Using Tags and Templates

1. Add a few different tags to your text, such as "To-Do," "Important," and "Question."
2. Explore available templates by clicking on "Insert" and selecting "Page Templates."
3. Apply a template to one of your pages, such as the "To-Do List" template.

Exercise 5: Collaboration and Sharing

1. Share your notebook with a friend or family member.
2. Collaborate on a page by having them add content or make edits.
3. Use the chat feature within OneNote to communicate with your collaborator while working on the same page.

Exercise 6: Using OneNote Web Clipper (Browser Extension)

1. Install the OneNote Web Clipper browser extension.
2. Visit a webpage and use the Web Clipper to capture a portion of the webpage, an entire article, or a bookmark.
3. Save the clipped content to your notebook.

Exercise 7: Drawing and Handwriting

1. Create a new page in your notebook.
2. Use the drawing tools to draw a simple doodle or write a short note using your mouse or touch screen.

Exercise 8: Optical Character Recognition (OCR)

1. Insert an image containing text into your notebook.
2. Right-click the image, select "Copy Text from Picture," and paste the copied text into a new page.

Exercise 9: Using Shortcuts

1. Familiarize yourself with common keyboard shortcuts like Ctrl+B (bold), Ctrl+I (italics), Ctrl+Z (undo), and Ctrl+Y (redo).
2. Try out shortcuts for creating new pages, sections, and notebooks.

Exercise 10: Practice Organization and Search

1. Create multiple pages and sections within your notebook, each dedicated to a different topic.
2. Use meaningful titles and tags to organize your content.
3. Try searching for specific notes using the search bar and see how quickly you can locate your information.

These exercises will help you get hands-on experience with the core features of OneNote and build your confidence as a beginner user. Remember that practice and exploration are key to mastering any new tool or software.

CONCLUSION

In conclusion, OneNote provides a versatile and user-friendly platform for beginners to dive into the realm of digital note-taking and organization. With its intuitive interface and features designed to enhance productivity, OneNote is a valuable tool for individuals looking to streamline their note-taking processes. Here's a summary of the key takeaways for beginners:

1. Seamless Note-Taking: OneNote offers a digital canvas where you can jot down notes, ideas, and information just as you would on paper. Its flexibility allows you to create text, draw, insert images, and more.

2. Organizational Power: The notebook-section-page hierarchy in OneNote ensures a structured approach to organizing your content. You can create multiple notebooks for different topics, sections for categories, and pages for specific notes.

3. Cross-Platform Accessibility: OneNote's synchronization capabilities enable you to access your notes across various devices, making it convenient to switch between your computer, tablet, and smartphone seamlessly.

4. Rich Formatting Options: Enjoy various formatting tools to make your notes visually appealing and easy to read. You can apply fonts, colors, styles, and even embed multimedia elements.

5. Collaboration and Sharing: OneNote facilitates collaboration by allowing you to share notebooks with others. You can invite colleagues, friends, or family members to work on notes in real-time.

6. Search and Organization: OneNote's powerful search function lets you quickly find specific notes, even within handwritten text and images. Tags and categories further enhance your ability to categorize and locate content.

7. Time-Saving Features: Utilize templates, tags, shortcuts, and Optical Character Recognition (OCR) to save time and enhance note-taking efficiency.

8. Learning Curve and Growth: While OneNote is accessible for beginners, there might be a learning curve as you explore its various features. Over time, you'll discover more ways to customize your notes and workflow.

9. Constant Improvement: Keep in mind that software updates might introduce new features and improvements to OneNote. Staying informed about updates can help you make the most of the application.

Starting your journey with OneNote as a beginner is an investment in efficient and organized note-taking. As you become more familiar with its functionalities, you'll uncover innovative ways to optimize your workflow and transform how you capture, store, and retrieve information. Whether you're a student, professional, or anyone seeking better organization, OneNote's beginner-friendly approach opens the door to enhanced productivity and creativity.

Thank you for your purchase! If you enjoyed this book, check out this other title. Happy reading!

Dear Reader, if you enjoyed reading my book, I would be very grateful if you could take a few moments to leave a review. Your feedback means a lot to me and will help others discover the book. Thank you so much for your support!

www.ingramcontent.com/pod-product-compliance
Lightning Source LLC
Chambersburg PA
CBHW062353290526
45794CB00005B/2200